Getting your Shell on
with PowerShell

By: Michael Neumann

Getting your Shell on
with PowerShell

By: Michael Neumann

Published by Mediaguruz Publishing at Mediaguruz.com

Getting your Shell on
with Powershell

Table of Contents

Introduction

Introduction to PowerShell and its evolution.

Understanding PowerShell
PowerShell is a versatile command-line shell and scripting language developed by Microsoft. It is designed primarily for system administration and automation. Unlike traditional command-line interfaces, PowerShell harnesses the power of .NET Framework, offering a more robust environment for automation and configuration management.

The Evolution of PowerShell
PowerShell has evolved significantly since its first release. Initially introduced as Windows PowerShell, it was exclusively for Windows operating systems. However, with the advent of PowerShell Core, now simply known as PowerShell, it has expanded its reach to include macOS and Linux platforms, embracing the cross-platform needs of modern IT environments. This evolution reflects a shift from a Windows-centric tool to a universal solution for system management across various platforms.

The Evolution of PowerShell: From PowerShell v1.0 to the Latest Version

These sections provide a comprehensive overview of PowerShell's development over the years and highlight its most impactful features and benefits.

PowerShell v1.0
- Released in 2006.
- Introduced the concept of Cmdlets, powerful, single-function commands.
- Laid the foundation for task automation and configuration management.

PowerShell v2.0
- Released in 2009.
- Brought advanced functions, modules, and remoting capabilities.
- Enhanced debugging and script execution policies for better security.

PowerShell v3.0
- Released in 2012.
- Improved workflow functions, enabling more complex automation scripts.
- Integrated with Windows Workflow Foundation for more robust automation solutions.

PowerShell v4.0
- Released in 2013.
- Introduced Desired State Configuration (DSC), a key feature for maintaining consistent system configurations.

PowerShell v5.0 and v5.1
- Released in 2015 and 2016.
- Expanded DSC capabilities and added class definitions in scripts.
- Improved module management and software installation via PowerShellGet.

PowerShell Core (v6)
- Released in 2018.
- Marked a major shift as it was rebuilt on .NET Core, enabling cross-platform support (Windows, Linux, macOS).
- Focused on open-source development and community-driven improvements.

PowerShell 7 and Beyond
- Combines the features of PowerShell Core and Windows PowerShell.
- Continues to evolve with ongoing community input and collaboration.
- Prioritizes cross-platform functionality and cloud-based scenarios.

Importance of PowerShell in modern IT infrastructure.

In today's complex IT environments, PowerShell stands out as an essential tool for system administrators and developers. Its ability to automate repetitive tasks, manage multiple systems simultaneously, and configure system settings makes it invaluable. PowerShell's integration with various Microsoft products, like Azure and Office 365, further cements its role in efficiently managing a wide array of technologies within an organization.

Overview of PowerShell's capabilities.

PowerShell's capabilities are extensive. It allows users to:

- Automate complex and repetitive tasks with scripting.
- Access and manipulate different types of data, such as XML, CSV, and JSON.
- Manage system resources like files, registries, and services efficiently.
- Interface with APIs and external programs for extended functionality.
- Remotely manage multiple systems, enhancing scalability and control.
- Create custom tools and utilities tailored to specific needs through its extensible framework.

PowerShell's combination of command-line speed, script flexibility, and deep integration with Windows and other platforms makes it a powerful tool for a wide range of tasks in modern IT infrastructure.

Key Features and Benefits of Using PowerShell

Automation of Repetitive Tasks
- Streamlines complex administrative tasks, reducing time and effort.
- Offers scripting capabilities to automate routine processes.

Cross-Platform Management
- PowerShell 7's cross-platform support enables management of systems across Windows, Linux, and macOS.
- Facilitates a unified approach to system administration in diverse environments.

Powerful Scripting Environment
- Combines command-line speed with the flexibility of scripting.
- Access to the full power of .NET classes and libraries.

Desired State Configuration (DSC)
- Automates the deployment and management of configuration data for software services and the environment on which these services run.

Robust Access to Data Stores
- Easily interfaces with various data formats like XML, JSON, and CSV.
- Simplifies data parsing and manipulation for administrative tasks.

Extensive Integration
- Integrates seamlessly with other Microsoft products and services.
- Offers a broad range of Cmdlets for managing Azure, Office 365, and other Microsoft technologies.

Community Support and Open Source
- Benefits from a large and active community.
- Open-source development model encourages innovation and rapid enhancement.

Chapter 1: Getting Started with PowerShell

This chapter provides you with an introductory overview of setting up and starting to use PowerShell. It covers the essentials of the PowerShell environment, its interface. This foundation is crucial for anyone beginning their journey with PowerShell.

Setting up the PowerShell environment.

Installation:
- Windows: PowerShell comes pre-installed in the most recent versions of Windows. For older versions or updates, download from the Microsoft website.
- macOS and Linux: Installation instructions vary by distribution. PowerShell can be installed via package managers like Homebrew or APT.

Launching PowerShell:
- Windows: Access PowerShell via the Start menu, or by typing **PowerShell** in the Run dialog.
- macOS/Linux: Open a terminal and type **pwsh**.

Configuration:
- Set execution policies to control the running of scripts (e.g., **Set-ExecutionPolicy RemoteSigned**).

- Customize the profile script for personalized startup configurations.

Understanding the PowerShell interface.

Command Line Interface (CLI):
- The primary interface for interacting with PowerShell.
- Users input commands, and PowerShell executes them and displays the output.

Integrated Scripting Environment (ISE):
- A GUI-based PowerShell editor available on Windows.
- Provides syntax highlighting, script debugging, and other advanced features.

Prompt Customization:
- Customize the PowerShell prompt to display additional information or improve usability.

Basic PowerShell syntax and commands.

Cmdlet Structure:
- Cmdlets are the primary command types in PowerShell.
- Syntax follows a **Verb-Noun** format, e.g., **Get-Help**, **Set-Location**.

Basic Cmdlets:
- **Get-Help**: Provides detailed information about PowerShell cmdlets.

- **Get-Command**: Lists all cmdlets, functions, workflows, etc., available to you.
- **Set-Location** and **Get-ChildItem**: Navigate and explore the file system.

Pipelines:
- Use the pipe symbol (**|**) to pass the output of one cmdlet as the input to another, e.g., **Get-Process | Where-Object {$_.CPU -gt 100}**.

Variables:
- Create and use variables to store data, e.g., **$myVariable = "Hello, PowerShell"**.

Script Execution:
- Learn how to run a script file (**.ps1**) and understand the basics of script security settings.

Chapter 2: PowerShell Scripting Basics

Introduction to scripting in PowerShell.

Defining PowerShell Scripts
- PowerShell scripts are essentially text files containing a sequence of PowerShell commands, known as cmdlets, along with variables, loops, conditionals, and functions. They are identified by the **.ps1** file extension and enable automating complex sequences of tasks, which are not possible with standalone commands.

The Role of Scripting in Automation
- Scripting is fundamental to automating repetitive tasks in PowerShell, allowing for complex data processing, system administration, and automation of routine IT operations.

Basic script creation and execution.

Writing Your First PowerShell Script
Objective: Create a script that lists all processes on a computer with CPU usage higher than 80%.

Script Structure:
- Begin with a **Get-Process** cmdlet to retrieve all running processes.

- Use a pipeline (|) to pass these processes to the **Where-Object** cmdlet.
- Filter processes where the CPU usage (**$_.CPU**) is greater than 80.
- Format the output for readability using **Format-Table -AutoSize**.

Example Script:

```
# This script lists processes with high CPU usage

Get-Process | Where-Object {$_.CPU -gt 80} | Format-Table -AutoSize
```

Comments: Use **#** to add comments and explain each part of the script for future reference and clarity.

Saving and Executing the Script
- Save the script with a **.ps1** extension, e.g., **HighCpuUsage.ps1**.
- To run the script, open PowerShell, navigate to the script's folder, and type **.\HighCpuUsage.ps1**.
- Ensure that your execution policy allows script execution.

Parameterizing Scripts
- Learn how to make scripts dynamic by passing parameters.

- Modify the script to accept a CPU threshold as a parameter.

Script safety and execution policies.

PowerShell Execution Policies
- Understand the different execution policies available in PowerShell, such as **Restricted**, **AllSigned**, **RemoteSigned**, and **Unrestricted**, and their implications on script security and usability.

Setting and Managing Execution Policies
- Use the **Set-ExecutionPolicy** cmdlet to define your script execution policy based on your security requirements and the trustworthiness of the scripts you intend to run.

Script Signing for Enhanced Security
- Learn the process of signing scripts with a digital certificate to ensure authenticity and integrity.
- Understand how to enforce a policy that only allows running signed scripts, especially in sensitive or high-security environments.

Security Best Practices
- Emphasize the importance of regular script audits and updates to mitigate vulnerabilities.
- Encourage testing scripts in a controlled environment before deployment.
- Educate users and administrators on the risks of running scripts from unverified sources.

Chapter 3: Working with PowerShell Cmdlets

Understanding cmdlets and their structure.

Introduction to Cmdlets
- Cmdlets, pronounced as "command-lets," are the fundamental building blocks of PowerShell. They are specialized .NET classes that implement specific functions, designed to be easy to use and remember.
- A cmdlet typically performs a small task, like managing services, reading files, or fetching network information.

Cmdlet Syntax
- PowerShell cmdlets follow a verb-noun naming convention. For instance, **Get-Content**, **Set-Date**, and **Remove-Item** are examples where the verb describes the action and the noun describes the resource to be acted upon.
- This structure makes cmdlets self-descriptive and helps in understanding their functionality.

Understanding Cmdlet Parameters
- Parameters are additional inputs that cmdlets can accept to modify their behavior. For example, **Get-ChildItem -Path C:\ -Recurse** uses the **-Path** and **-Recurse** parameters.

- Parameters can be mandatory or optional, with some cmdlets having default parameters.

Commonly used cmdlets.

File and Directory Operations
- **Get-ChildItem**: Lists items in a directory.
- **Copy-Item, Move-Item, Remove-Item**: Used for copying, moving, and deleting files or directories.

System Administration
- **Get-Service, Start-Service, Stop-Service**: Manage Windows services.
- **Get-Process**: Retrieve and manipulate processes running on the system.

Text and Data Handling
- **Get-Content, Set-Content**: Read and write data to files.
- **ConvertTo-Json, ConvertFrom-Json**: Convert data to and from JSON format.

Network Interaction
- **Test-Connection**: Similar to the ping command, used to test network connectivity.
- **Invoke-WebRequest**: Fetch data from the web.

Finding and using cmdlets with Get-Help.

Leveraging Get-Help
- **Get-Help** is a fundamental cmdlet in PowerShell to learn about other cmdlets. It provides detailed information, including syntax, parameters, examples, and links to more detailed help.
- Usage: **Get-Help <Cmdlet-Name>** – for example, **Get-Help Get-Process**.

Exploring Cmdlets with Get-Help
- Detailed View: Use **Get-Help <Cmdlet-Name> -Detailed** for an in-depth look at a cmdlet's usage.
- Examples: The **-Examples** flag shows practical examples of how to use a cmdlet.
- Online Help: The **-Online** parameter opens the most updated help page in a web browser.

Using Get-Command
- **Get-Command** is another valuable tool. It lists all cmdlets, functions, workflows, and scripts available to the user, providing a way to discover new cmdlets.
- Filter cmdlets using **Get-Command -Verb <Verb>** or **Get-Command -Noun <Noun>** to find specific actions or resources.

Conclusion

This chapter has introduced the core elements of PowerShell's cmdlets, their syntax, and how to use

Get-Help to understand and find cmdlets effectively. Understanding these concepts is vital for anyone looking to harness the power of PowerShell for scripting and automation.

Chapter 4: PowerShell Pipeline and Object Manipulation

Understanding the pipeline concept.

Introduction to the Pipeline
- The PowerShell pipeline is a key feature that sets it apart from traditional shells. It allows users to pass objects, not just text, from one cmdlet to another. This enables efficient data manipulation and reduces resource usage.
- In essence, the pipeline connects multiple cmdlets in a sequence where the output of one cmdlet becomes the input to the next.

How the Pipeline Works
- PowerShell processes the pipeline from left to right. Each cmdlet in the pipeline performs an operation and passes its output forward.
- This operation is efficient because PowerShell sends objects through the pipeline as soon as they are available, rather than waiting for the entire operation to be completed.

Using the pipeline to manipulate objects.

Object-Based Nature of PowerShell

- PowerShell works with objects — structured data that is more than just strings or text. Each object can have properties and methods, allowing for sophisticated manipulation and control.

Practical Pipeline Usage
- Example: The command **Get-Process | Sort-Object CPU -Descending | Select-Object -First 5** takes process objects, sorts them by CPU usage in descending order, and then selects the first five.
- These cmdlets work together seamlessly, handling complex data operations with minimal code.

Filtering and sorting data in the pipeline.

Filtering with Where-Object
- **Where-Object** is a powerful cmdlet used for filtering data in the pipeline. It allows you to specify conditions to filter out objects.
- Example: **Get-Service | Where-Object { $_.Status -eq 'Running' }** filters services that are currently running.

Sorting with Sort-Object
- **Sort-Object** sorts objects in ascending or descending order based on object properties.

- Usage: **Get-EventLog -LogName Application | Sort-Object TimeGenerated -Descending** sorts application events in reverse chronological order.

Advanced Manipulations
- Combining cmdlets for advanced data manipulation, like grouping and comparing objects.
- Example: **Get-Process | Group-Object - Property ProcessName** groups processes by their names.

Conclusion

This chapter delves into the powerful concept of the PowerShell pipeline, highlighting its efficiency in handling objects and enabling sophisticated data manipulation. Understanding and effectively using the pipeline is a crucial skill for PowerShell users, greatly enhancing the ability to process and analyze data.

Chapter 5: PowerShell Providers and Drives

Introduction to providers and drives.

Understanding Providers in PowerShell
- Providers in PowerShell are powerful mechanisms that allow access to various data stores as if they were file systems. These data stores include the file system, the registry, and more.
- A provider acts like a bridge, translating the data store's native commands and data structures into a set of standard commands that PowerShell understands.

Concept of Drives in PowerShell
- PowerShell uses a drive-based system to access different data stores. These drives are not limited to physical disk drives but extend to other data stores like the Registry, Certificates, and Environment Variables.
- Drives in PowerShell are accessed similarly to file system drives, using familiar commands like **cd**, **dir**, and **copy**.

Working with file system, registry, and other drives.

File System Drive

- The most commonly used drive, typically represented as **C:**, **D:**, etc.
- Operations include navigating directories, manipulating files, and retrieving file information.

Registry Drive

- Accessed via the **HKLM:** and **HKCU:** drives for HKEY_LOCAL_MACHINE and HKEY_CURRENT_USER, respectively.
- Enables viewing and editing registry keys and values, crucial for system configuration and troubleshooting.

Other PowerShell Drives

- **Env:**: Accesses environment variables.
- **Cert:**: Manages certificates stored on your system.
- Custom drives can be created for specific data stores using PowerShell's provider functionality.

Navigating and manipulating data with providers.

Basic Navigation
- Use standard commands like **Set-Location** (**cd**), **Get-ChildItem** (**dir**), and **Get-Item** to navigate and explore different drives.
- Example: **Set-Location HKLM:** to navigate into the Registry's Local Machine hive.

Data Manipulation
- Create, modify, and delete items within drives using cmdlets like **New-Item**, **Set-Item**, **Remove-Item**.
- Handle specific data types appropriately, such as strings in the file system and key/value pairs in the registry.

Advanced Provider Features
- Providers support advanced features like transactions in the registry provider, allowing for rollback of changes.
- Explore provider-specific capabilities like accessing the digital signature of files or viewing certificate details.

Conclusion
This chapter introduces PowerShell providers and drives, key concepts that extend PowerShell's versatility beyond traditional shell environments. Understanding how to navigate and manipulate different types of data stores through PowerShell's uniform interface significantly broadens the scope of administrative and scripting tasks that can be efficiently managed.

Chapter 6: Variables, Data Types, and Operators

Working with variables in PowerShell.

Introduction to Variables
- Variables in PowerShell are used to store data that can be used and manipulated throughout a script. They are prefixed with a dollar sign ($), e.g., **$myVariable**.
- Variables can store various types of data, including strings, integers, arrays, and even complex objects.

Creating and Using Variables
- Assigning values to variables: **$myVariable = 'Hello, PowerShell'**.
- Accessing variable values by simply referencing the variable name.
- Variables are dynamically typed, meaning their type is determined by the value they are assigned.

Scope of Variables
- Understanding local, global, and script scopes.
- Techniques for modifying variable scope, for instance, using the **global:** and **script:** scope modifiers.

Understanding data types and operators.

Common Data Types
- Basic types: Strings (**[string]**), Integers (**[int]**), Booleans (**[bool]**).
- Complex types: Arrays, HashTables, Custom Objects.
- Special types: **PSObject**, which represents objects in PowerShell.

Operators in PowerShell
- Arithmetic operators: **+**, **-**, *****, **/**, **%**.
- Comparison operators: **-eq**, **-ne**, **-gt**, **-lt**, **-ge**, **-le**.
- Logical operators: **-and**, **-or**, **-not**.

Understanding Type Casting
- Explicitly converting data types, e.g., **[int]'123'**.
- PowerShell's ability to automatically cast types where necessary.

Type conversions and manipulations.

Working with Type Conversions
- Methods for explicit type conversion.
- Handling type conversion errors and exceptions.

Manipulating Complex Types
- Techniques for working with arrays: indexing, slicing, adding, and removing elements.
- Handling associative arrays or hash tables: creating, adding key-value pairs, accessing, and modifying values.

Advanced Data Manipulations
- Creating custom objects and adding properties to objects.
- Using type accelerators for quick reference to common .NET types.

Conclusion
This chapter delves into the fundamental concepts of variables, data types, and operators in PowerShell. It provides the groundwork for understanding how to store, manipulate, and manage data effectively in PowerShell scripts. This knowledge is essential for scripting and effectively working with PowerShell to automate complex tasks.

Chapter 7: Control Flow and Looping Constructs

Conditional statements in PowerShell.

Basics of Conditional Logic
- Conditional statements allow scripts to make decisions based on the value of variables or expressions.
- The primary conditional statement in PowerShell is **if**, which can be combined with **else** and **elseif** for more complex logic.

Using if, else, and elseif
- Syntax and examples of using **if** statements to execute code blocks conditionally.
- Nesting **else** and **elseif** statements for multiple conditions.
- Best practices for writing clear and efficient conditional logic.

Example Time-Based Greeting PowerShell Script Example: Time-Based Greeting

```
# Get the current hour

$currentHour = (Get-Date).Hour

# Check the current hour and output a greeting
```

```powershell
if ($currentHour -lt 12) {

    # If the hour is less than 12, it's morning

    Write-Host "Good morning!"

} elseif ($currentHour -lt 18) {

    # If the hour is less than 18 but greater than or
equal to 12, it's afternoon

    Write-Host "Good afternoon!"

} else {

    # If the hour is 18 or later, it's evening

    Write-Host "Good evening!"

}
```

How This Script Works:

1. **Get the Current Hour**: The script starts by retrieving the current hour using **Get-Date**. The **.Hour** property extracts the hour component from the current time.

2. **Conditional Logic**:
   - The **if** statement checks if the current hour is less than 12. If true, it outputs "Good morning!"
   - The **elseif** statement is evaluated next. If the current hour is less than 18 (but didn't satisfy the first **if** condition), it outputs "Good afternoon!"

- Finally, the **else** statement covers all remaining scenarios, which in this case is any time 18:00 (6 PM) or later, outputting "Good evening!"

This script is a basic example of how conditional statements can be used in PowerShell to perform different actions based on certain conditions—in this case, the time of day.

Looping constructs: for, foreach, while, do-while.

The for Loop
- Explanation of the **for** loop structure: initialization, condition, and increment.
- Use cases and examples of iterating over a set of values or a range of numbers.

*Example **For Loop** - Counting Numbers*

```
# For loop to count from 1 to 5
for ($i = 1; $i -le 5; $i++) {
 Write-Host "Counting: $i"
}
```

This script uses a **for** loop to count from 1 to 5. The loop initializes **$i** to 1, continues as long as **$i** is less than or equal to 5, and increments **$i** by 1 in each iteration.

foreach Loop
- Designed for iterating over collections like arrays or lists.
- Simpler syntax compared to **for**, automatically handles the iteration over each element in a collection.

*Example **Foreach Loop** - Iterating Over an Array*

```
# Array of names
$names = @("Alice", "Bob", "Charlie")

# Foreach loop to iterate over each name
foreach ($name in $names) {
    Write-Host "Hello, $name!"
}
```

This script creates an array of names and uses a **foreach** loop to iterate over each element. For each name in the array, it prints a greeting.

The while and do-while Loops

- **while** loops: Execute a block of code as long as a specified condition is true.
- **do-while** loops: Similar to **while**, but ensures the code block is executed at least once.

```
# While loop to repeat until a certain
condition is met

$counter = 1

while ($counter -le 3) {

    Write-Host "Loop iteration: $counter"

    $counter++

}
```

The **while** loop in this script keeps running as long as the **$counter** variable is less than or equal to 3. Each iteration increases the **$counter** by 1.

*Example **Do-While Loop** - Executing At Least Once*

```
# Do-while loop to execute the block at
least once

$counter = 1

do {

Write-Host "This loop will run at least once.
Counter: $counter"

counter++

} while ($counter -le 5)
```

This **do-while** loop ensures that the code block executes at least once, regardless of the condition. The loop runs while **$counter** is less than or equal to 5.

Explanation of Each Loop:

- **For Loop**: Ideal for scenarios where you know in advance how many times you need to iterate.
- **Foreach Loop**: Best suited for iterating over collections like arrays or lists.
- **While Loop**: Useful when you want to repeat an action until a certain condition becomes false.
- **Do-While Loop**: Similar to the **while** loop, but guarantees that the loop's body executes at least once.

Using break and continue.

Control Loop Execution with break and continue.

- **break**: Immediately exits the loop, skipping any remaining iterations.
- **continue**: Skips the current iteration and moves to the next one.
- Scenarios and examples illustrating the use of **break** and **continue** in controlling loop flow.

Nested Loops and Control Statements

- Handling **break** and **continue** in nested loops.
- Strategies for managing complex looping scenarios and avoiding common pitfalls.

Conclusion

This chapter provides an in-depth exploration of control flow and looping constructs in PowerShell. Understanding these constructs is crucial for writing scripts that can perform repetitive tasks efficiently and make decisions based on dynamic conditions. The knowledge of how to effectively use conditional statements and loops is foundational for any PowerShell scripter.

Chapter 8: Advanced Data Manipulation

Working with arrays and hash tables.

Introduction to Arrays
- Arrays in PowerShell are used to store a collection of items. They can be of mixed data types and dynamically increase in size.
- Creating arrays, accessing elements, and array operations like adding, removing, and sorting elements.

Example Array

```
# Creating an array with initial
elements
$myArray = @(1, 2, 3, 4, 5)

# Adding elements to the array
$myArray += 6
$myArray += 7, 8

# Accessing specific elements
$thirdElement = $myArray[2]  #        Arrays
are zero-indexed
Write-Host "The third element is:
$thirdElement"

# Iterating over the array
Write-Host "Iterating over the array:"
```

```
foreach ($element in $myArray) {
 Write-Host $element
}

# Counting the elements in the array
$arrayCount = $myArray.Count
Write-Host "The array has     $arrayCount
elements."
```

How This Script Works:

1. **Array Creation**: The script starts by creating an array named **$myArray** with initial elements (1, 2, 3, 4, 5).
2. **Adding Elements**: New elements (6, 7, 8) are added to the array using the **+=** operator.
3. **Accessing Elements**: The script demonstrates how to access a specific element, in this case, the third element (index 2 since arrays are zero-indexed).
4. **Iteration**: A **foreach** loop is used to iterate through each element in the array, printing each element to the console.
5. **Counting Elements**: Finally, the script counts the number of elements in the array using the **.Count** property and displays this count.

This example gives a basic overview of array operations in PowerShell, showcasing their flexibility and utility in scripts. Arrays are fundamental for storing and manipulating collections of data in PowerShell.

Advanced Array Techniques

- Multi-dimensional arrays: Creating and accessing.
- Array filtering and processing using cmdlets and pipeline operations.

Example Listing Specific Files and Output to a Text File

```
# Define the directory to search and the file type
$directoryPath = "C:\YourDirectory"  # Replace with your directory path
$fileExtension = "*.txt"  # Replace with the desired file extension

# Get all files with the specified extension in the directory and its subdirectories
$files = Get-ChildItem -Path $directoryPath -Recurse -Filter $fileExtension

# Define the output file path
$outputFilePath = "C:\YourOutputDirectory\fileList.txt"

# Write the full path of each file to the output file
foreach ($file in $files) {
    $file.FullName | Out-File -Append -FilePath $outputFilePath
}
```

```
# Display a completion message
Write-Host "File list has been saved to
$outputFilePath"
```

How This Script Works:

1. **Directory and File Type**: The script starts by defining the directory path (**$directoryPath**) where you want to search for files and the type of files you're looking for (**$fileExtension**). You should replace **"C:\YourDirectory"** and **"*.txt"** with your desired directory and file extension.
2. **Searching for Files**: It uses **Get-ChildItem** to search for all files in the specified directory and its subdirectories that match the file extension. The results are stored in the **$files** array.
3. **Output File Path**: The path for the output file is defined in **$outputFilePath**. This is where the script will write the names of the found files. Replace **"C:\YourOutputDirectory\fileList.txt"** with your desired output file path.
4. **Writing to the Output File**: The script iterates over each file found and writes the full path of the file to the output file using **Out-File**.
5. **Completion Message**: Finally, the script prints a message to the console to indicate that the

operation is complete and where the file list is saved.

This script is a simple yet practical example of using PowerShell to automate a common task: searching for files of a specific type and saving the results to a file. It demonstrates file system interaction, array handling, and basic output operations in PowerShell.

Understanding Hash Tables
- Hash tables store data in key-value pairs and are excellent for storing and retrieving data where each item has a unique key.
- Creating hash tables, adding/removing key-value pairs, and accessing values.

Example Hash Table Script

```
# Creating a hash table
$myHashTable = @{}

# Adding key-value pairs to the hash table
$myHashTable["name"] = "John Doe"
$myHashTable["age"] = 30
$myHashTable["email"] =
"john.doe@example.com"

# Displaying the entire hash table
Write-Host "Initial hash table:"
$myHashTable

# Accessing a specific value by key
Write-Host "Name: " $myHashTable["name"]
```

```
# Modifying a value
$myHashTable["email"] =
"johndoe@newdomain.com"
Write-Host "Updated email: "
$myHashTable["email"]

# Removing a key-value pair
$myHashTable.Remove("age")
Write-Host "Hash table after removing
'age':"
$myHashTable

# Adding a new key-value pair
$myHashTable["department"] = "IT"
Write-Host "Hash table after adding
'department':"
$myHashTable
```

How This Script Works:

1. **Create Hash Table**: The script starts by creating an empty hash table **$myHashTable**.
2. **Add Key-Value Pairs**: It then adds several key-value pairs to the hash table, representing a person's name, age, and email.
3. **Display Hash Table**: The script prints the entire hash table to the console.
4. **Access Specific Value**: Demonstrates how to retrieve a value using its key (e.g., **$myHashTable["name"]**).

5. **Modify Value**: The script updates the value associated with the "email" key.
6. **Remove Key-Value Pair**: Demonstrates how to remove a key-value pair using the **.Remove** method.
7. **Add New Key-Value Pair**: Finally, it adds a new key-value pair to the hash table.

Hash tables are a versatile and powerful data structure in PowerShell, ideal for storing related data in key-value pairs. This script demonstrates their fundamental operations, providing a basic understanding of how to use them in PowerShell scripting.

Manipulating Hash Tables

- Advanced operations like merging hash tables, iterating over keys and values, and handling collisions.

Example Script: Advanced Hash Table Manipulation

```
# Creating two hash tables
$hashTable1 = @{
    "Name" = "Alice";
    "Age" = 28;
    "Email" = "alice@example.com"
}
$hashTable2 = @{
    "Department" = "IT";
    "Location" = "New York";
    "Email" = "alice.work@example.com"  # Intentional collision for demonstration
}

# Merging hash tables
```

```powershell
# Note: In case of key collisions, values from
the second hash table will overwrite  those
from the first

$mergedHashTable = $hashTable1.Clone()

foreach ($key in $hashTable2.Keys) {

  $mergedHashTable[$key] =
$hashTable2[$key]

}


Write-Host "Merged Hash Table:"

$mergedHashTable


# Iterating over keys and values

Write-Host "Iterating over merged hash
table:"

foreach ($key in $mergedHashTable.Keys) {

  $value = $mergedHashTable[$key]

  Write-Host "$key: $value"

}


# Handling collisions (simple example)

# Checking if a key exists before adding or
modifying it
```

```
$collisionKey = "Email"

if ($hashTable1.ContainsKey($collisionKey)) {

    Write-Host "Collision detected for key:
    $collisionKey. Original value: $
    ($hashTable1[$collisionKey]). New value:
    $($hashTable2[$collisionKey])"

    # Handling collision: Choose to keep the
    original, update, or merge values

    # Example: Keeping the original value

    # $mergedHashTable[$collisionKey] =
    $hashTable1[$collisionKey]

}
```

How This Script Works:

1. **Create Hash Tables**: Two hash tables, **$hashTable1**
   and **$hashTable2**, are created with different key-
   value pairs. There's an intentional collision on the
   "Email" key for demonstration purposes.
2. **Merge Hash Tables**: The script merges
   $hashTable2 into **$hashTable1**. In the case of key
   collisions, values from **$hashTable2** overwrite those
   from **$hashTable1**. This is achieved by first cloning
   $hashTable1 and then iterating over **$hashTable2**
   to either add new keys or update existing ones.

3. **Iterate Over Hash Table**: The script demonstrates how to iterate over keys and values in the merged hash table.
4. **Handle Collisions**: Before merging, the script checks for collisions. If a collision is detected (same key in both hash tables), it's handled as per the logic you define. In this script, it simply outputs a message indicating the collision and the differing values. You can choose to keep either value or merge them as needed.

This example provides insights into some of the more advanced operations you can perform with hash tables in PowerShell, including merging tables and handling collisions. These techniques are particularly useful in scenarios where you need to combine data from multiple sources or handle complex data structures.

Advanced string manipulation.

- **String Operations**
  - Basic string functions: concatenation, substring, replacement, and formatting.
  - Regular expressions for pattern matching and complex replacements.

Example String Operations

```
# String concatenation

$string1 = "Hello, "

$string2 = "PowerShell!"

$concatenatedString = $string1 + $string2

Write-Host "Concatenated String: $concatenatedString"


# Substring

$substring = $concatenatedString.Substring(7, 10)

Write-Host "Substring: $substring"


# String replacement
```

```powershell
$replacedString =
$concatenatedString.Replace("PowerShell",
"World")

Write-Host "Replaced String:
$replacedString"


# String formatting

$name = "Alice"

$age = 30

$formattedString = "Name: {0}, Age: {1}" -f
$name, $age

Write-Host "Formatted String:
$formattedString"


# Regular Expressions - Pattern Matching
and Replacements

$regexString = "The rain in Spain stays
mainly in the plain."

# Pattern match

if ($regexString -match "Spain") {

   Write-Host "The string contains 'Spain'."

}
```

```
# Complex replacement using regex

$replacedRegexString =
[regex]::Replace($regexString, "ain",
"ain(FOUND)")

Write-Host "Replaced Regex String:
$replacedRegexString"
```

How This Script Works:
1. **String Concatenation**: Combines **$string1** and **$string2** using the + operator.
2. **Substring**: Extracts a part of the string starting at the 8th character (index 7) and spanning 10 characters.
3. **String Replacement**: Replaces the word "PowerShell" with "World" in the concatenated string.
4. **String Formatting**: Uses the **-f** operator to format a string with variables **$name** and **$age**.
5. **Regular Expressions**:
   - **Pattern Matching**: Checks if **$regexString** contains the word "Spain" using the **-match** operator.
   - **Complex Replacement**: Uses a regular expression to find all occurrences of "ain" and appends "(FOUND)" to each occurrence.

This example demonstrates various ways to manipulate and work with strings in PowerShell, showcasing fundamental string operations and the power of regular expressions for more complex text processing tasks.

- **PowerShell and Regular Expressions**
  - Using PowerShell's **-match**, **-replace**, and other regex-based operators.
  - Complex pattern matching and text processing using regular expressions.

Example Using Regular Expressions

```
# Sample text

$text = "Emails: john.doe@example.com, jane.smith@workplace.org"


# Pattern matching with -match

# Check if the text contains an email address

$emailPattern = "\b[A-Za-z0-9._%+-]+@[A-Za-z0-9.-]+\.[A-Z|a-z]{2,}\b"

if ($text -match $emailPattern) {

    Write-Host "Email found: $($Matches[0])"

} else {
```

```powershell
    Write-Host "No email found."

}


# Extracting all email addresses using -
match and regex

$matches = [regex]::Matches($text,
$emailPattern)

$emails = $matches | ForEach-Object {
$_.Value }

Write-Host "All emails found: $($emails -join
', ')"


# Using -replace with regex for complex
replacements

# Example: Masking email addresses

$maskedEmailText = [regex]::Replace($text,
$emailPattern, '***@***.***')

Write-Host "Masked Emails:
$maskedEmailText"


# Splitting text using -split with regex

# Splitting text into words

$words = $text -split "\s+"
```

```
Write-Host "Words in the text: $($words -
join ', ')"
```

How This Script Works

1. **Pattern Matching with -match**: The script first
   checks if the **$text** contains an email address using
   the **-match** operator with a regex pattern for email.
   If a match is found, it outputs the first email
   address.
2. **Extracting All Matches**: Using **[regex]::Matches**,
   the script extracts all occurrences of email
   addresses from the text and lists them.
3. **Complex Replacement with -replace**: The script
   then uses **[regex]::Replace** to mask the email
   addresses in the text, demonstrating how to
   perform complex replacements using regex.
4. **Splitting Text with -split**: Finally, the script uses
   the **-split** operator with a regex pattern to split the
   text into individual words.

This script demonstrates the versatility of regular
expressions in PowerShell for tasks like pattern
matching, extracting specific data, complex
replacements, and text splitting. Regular expressions
are incredibly powerful for text processing and are an
essential tool in any PowerShell scripter's toolbox.

Custom object creation and manipulation.

- **Creating Custom Objects**
    - Methods to create custom objects, such as **New-Object** and PSCustomObject (**[pscustomobject]@{}**).
    - Adding, modifying, and removing properties from custom objects.

Creating a Custom Object with New-Object

```
# Creating a custom object using New-Object

$person = New-Object -TypeName PSObject

$person | Add-Member -MemberType NoteProperty -Name "Name" -Value "John Doe"

$person | Add-Member -MemberType NoteProperty -Name "Age" -Value 30

$person | Add-Member -MemberType NoteProperty -Name "Email" -Value "john.doe@example.com"


# Display the custom object

Write-Host "Custom Object using New-Object:"

$person
```

Creating with New-Object: The script starts by creating a custom object named **$person** using **New-Object - TypeName PSObject**. It then adds properties (**Name**, **Age**, **Email**) to the object using **Add-Member**.

Creating a Custom Object with PSCustomObject

```
# Creating a custom object using PSCustomObject
$employee = [PSCustomObject]@{
    Name = "Jane Smith"
  Position = "Developer"
    Department = "IT"
}


# Display the custom object
Write-Host "Custom Object using PSCustomObject:"
$employee
```

Creating with PSCustomObject: It also demonstrates creating another custom object, **$employee**, using a hashtable and casting it to **[PSCustomObject]**.

- **Manipulating Objects**
  - Object methods: exploring and using the methods associated with objects.
  - Sorting, filtering, and comparing custom objects.

- **Advanced Object Concepts**
  - Deep dive into object properties, methods, and their applications in scripting.
  - Working with object types and casts in complex scenarios.

Conclusion

Chapter 8 guides you through advanced techniques in data manipulation within PowerShell. It covers the intricacies of arrays, hash tables, string manipulation, and custom objects. Mastery of these topics allows for more sophisticated and powerful scripting, enabling users to handle complex data structures and perform intricate data operations efficiently in PowerShell.

Chapter 9: Functions and Script Modules

Writing functions in PowerShell.

- **Introduction to Functions**
    - Functions in PowerShell are reusable blocks of code designed to perform a specific task.
    - Basic structure of a PowerShell function includes the **Function** keyword, a name, and a code block.

- **Creating a Simple Function**

    - Example of a basic function:

```
function Get-Greeting {

    param ($name)

    "Hello, $name!"

}


# Calling the function

Get-Greeting -name "Alice"
```

Return Values

- Functions can return values using the `Return` keyword or by outputting values directly.

Scope of variables and function parameters.

- **Variable Scope**
  - Understanding local, script, and global scopes in PowerShell.
  - How variables behave differently inside and outside of functions.

- **Function Parameters**
  - Defining and using parameters in functions.
  - Parameter types: mandatory, optional, and positional parameters.

Example with Scoped Variables and Parameters

- Demonstrating variable scope and parameter usage:

```
function Set-GlobalValue {

param ($value)

 $script:globalValue = $value

}
Set-GlobalValue -value "Shared Data"

Write-Host "Global Value: $globalValue"
```

Creating and using script modules.

- **What are Script Modules?**
  - Script modules are a collection of functions saved in a **.psm1** file.
  - They allow for code reusability and distribution.

- **Creating a Script Module**
  - Steps to write and save a script module.
  - Example module content (**MyModule.psm1**):

```
function Get-TimeString {

Get-Date -Format "hh:mm:ss"

}



Export-ModuleMember -Function Get-TimeString
```

- **Using Script Modules**
  - Importing a module with **Import-Module**.
  - Accessing functions from the module.

- **Module Example**
  - Using the **Get-TimeString** function from **MyModule.psm1**:

```
Import-Module ./MyModule.psm1

Get-TimeString
```

Conclusion

Chapter 9 provides a comprehensive guide to writing functions and creating script modules in PowerShell. It covers the basics of function structure, variable scope, parameter handling, and the steps to create reusable script modules. These concepts are essential for organizing and structuring PowerShell code effectively, especially in complex scripting scenarios.

Chapter 10: Error Handling and Debugging

In this chapter, we're diving deep into the world of error handling and debugging in PowerShell. These are critical skills for any PowerShell user, enabling you to write more robust and reliable scripts. We'll explore the different types of errors you might encounter, how to handle them effectively, and various debugging techniques to troubleshoot your scripts.

Understanding error types in PowerShell.

In this section, we delve into the different types of errors you might encounter while working with PowerShell. Errors in PowerShell are broadly classified into two categories: **Terminating** and **Non-Terminating** errors.

- **Terminating Errors**: These are critical errors that halt the execution of a script. They occur in situations where further execution could lead to data loss or corruption. For example, an attempt to divide by zero.

- **Non-Terminating Errors**: These errors do not stop the script from executing. They usually occur in less critical situations, like trying to access a file that does not exist.

Example

```
# Non-Terminating Error

Get-Item "non_existent_file.txt"


# Terminating Error

$result = 1 / 0
```

Implementing try-catch-finally blocks.

To manage errors effectively, PowerShell provides the **try-catch-finally** construct. This structure allows you to handle errors gracefully and execute code regardless of whether an error occurred.

- **Try Block**: Contains the code that may cause an error.
- **Catch Block**: Executes if an error occurs in the try block.
- **Finally Block**: Executes regardless of whether an error occurred, often used for cleanup tasks.

Example:

```
try {
    $content = Get-Content "config.txt"
} catch {
    Write-Host "Error: $_"
} finally {
    Write-Host "Execution completed."
}
```

Debugging scripts in PowerShell.

Debugging is an essential skill for any PowerShell scripter. This section covers tools and techniques for effective debugging.

- **Using Breakpoints**: Set breakpoints in your script to pause execution and inspect variables.
- **Write-Debug Command**: Insert **Write-Debug** statements in your script to output debugging information.
- **PowerShell ISE**: Use the Integrated Scripting Environment for an interactive debugging experience.

Example

```
$i = 0

while ($i -lt 10) {
    Write-Debug "Current value of i: $i"
    # ... rest of the code
    $i++
}
```

By the end of this chapter, you'll have a solid understanding of how to handle errors in PowerShell and debug your scripts effectively, ensuring more reliable and robust PowerShell

Chapter 11: Working with Files and Folders

This chapter provides an in-depth guide to managing files and folders in PowerShell. From basic manipulations like creating and deleting files, to advanced operations such as content searching and file comparison, this chapter aims to equip you with the skills to effectively handle file system tasks using PowerShell.

File and folder manipulation using PowerShell.

This section introduces the basic PowerShell cmdlets used for creating, deleting, moving, and renaming files and folders.

- **Creating Files and Folders**: Use **New-Item** to create new files and directories.
- **Deleting Files and Folders**: **Remove-Item** allows you to delete files and directories.
- **Moving and Renaming**: **Move-Item** and **Rename-Item** are used for moving and renaming files and folders, respectively.

Example

```
# Creating a new directory
New-Item -Path "C:\MyFolder" -ItemType Directory


# Creating a new file
New-Item -Path "C:\MyFolder\MyFile.txt" -ItemType File


# Moving the file to a new location
Move-Item -Path "C:\MyFolder\MyFile.txt" -Destination "C:\NewFolder"


# Renaming the file
Rename-Item -Path "C:\NewFolder\MyFile.txt" -NewName "NewFile.txt"
```

Reading from and writing to files.

Learn how to interact with the content of files using PowerShell. This includes reading data from files and writing or appending data to files.

- **Reading Files**: Use `Get-Content` to read the contents of a file.
- **Writing to Files**: `Set-Content` and `Add-Content` are used to write or append data to a file.

Example

```
# Reading from a file

$content = Get-Content "C:\MyFolder\MyFile.txt"


# Writing to a file

Set-Content -Path "C:\MyFolder\MyFile.txt" -Value "New Content"


# Appending to a file

Add-Content -Path "C:\MyFolder\MyFile.txt" -Value "Additional Content"
```

Advanced file operations like search and comparison.

This part covers more advanced file operations like searching within files and comparing file contents.

- **Searching in Files**: Use **Select-String** for pattern matching and text searching within files.

- **Comparing Files**: **Compare-Object** can be used to compare the content of two files.

Example

```
# Searching for a specific text in files

Get-ChildItem -Path "C:\MyFolder\" -Recurse |
Select-String -Pattern "SearchText"


# Comparing two files

$file1 = Get-Content "C:\MyFolder\File1.txt"

$file2 = Get-Content "C:\MyFolder\File2.txt"

Compare-Object -ReferenceObject $file1 -
DifferenceObject $file2
```

Conclusion

By the end of this chapter, you will have a thorough understanding of file and folder manipulation in PowerShell. These skills are fundamental for automating and streamlining tasks, managing data, and maintaining an organized file system. Whether you're starting in PowerShell or seeking to enhance your scripting abilities, this chapter provides the foundational knowledge and advanced techniques for effective file system management.

Chapter 12: PowerShell Remoting and Script Execution

In this chapter, we delve into the powerful capabilities of PowerShell in the realm of remoting and script execution. PowerShell remoting enables administrators and scripters to run commands and scripts on remote computers, a critical feature for managing a network of machines. This chapter covers the essentials of setting up and using remote sessions, as well as key security considerations for script execution

- Understanding PowerShell remoting.

   Introduction to Remoting: PowerShell Remoting, using the WS-Management protocol, allows for running commands on remote systems. This feature is crucial for managing multiple machines or executing tasks remotely.
- **Enabling Remoting**: Before you can use remoting, it must be enabled on both the local and remote machines. The **Enable-PSRemoting** cmdlet is used to configure a computer to accept remote PowerShell sessions.

Example

```
# Enable PowerShell Remoting on a local
computer
Enable-PSRemoting -Force
```

- **The Use of WinRM**: Windows Remote Management (WinRM) is the underlying service for PowerShell remoting. Understanding and configuring WinRM is crucial for secure and efficient remoting.

Setting up and using remote sessions.

Creating Remote Sessions: The **New-PSSession** cmdlet is used to create a remote PowerShell session. Sessions can be saved and reused, reducing the overhead of creating new connections.

Example

```
# Creating a new remote session

$session = New-PSSession -ComputerName "Server01" -Credential (Get-    Credential)
```

- **Executing Commands Remotely**: Once a session is established, **Invoke-Command** can be used to run commands on the remote machine. This cmdlet is versatile and can be used for a wide range of remote operations.

Example

```
# Executing a command on a remote machine

Invoke-Command -Session $session -ScriptBlock { Get-Process }
```

Security considerations for script execution.

- **Execution Policies**: Understand the role of execution policies in PowerShell and how they help in controlling the running of scripts. The **Set-ExecutionPolicy** cmdlet is key in managing these policies.
- **Securing Credentials and Sessions**: Handling credentials securely is paramount in remote sessions. Techniques like using secure strings and encrypted sessions are discussed.
- **Best Practices for Secure Remoting**: This section covers the best practices for secure remoting, including using HTTPS for WinRM, setting up proper firewall rules, and auditing remote sessions.

Conclusion

Mastering PowerShell remoting and understanding the security implications of script execution are fundamental skills for any professional working in a Windows environment. By the end of this chapter, you will be equipped with the knowledge to set up, manage, and secure PowerShell remote sessions, ensuring efficient and secure management of your networked resources. This expertise is vital for system administrators, IT professionals, and anyone responsible for managing a Windows-based infrastructure.

Chapter 13: Using PowerShell with Microsoft Technologies

This chapter offers an insightful exploration into the integration of PowerShell with various Microsoft technologies. PowerShell, being a powerful scripting language developed by Microsoft, is inherently designed to work seamlessly with a host of Microsoft products and services. From managing Windows Server environments to automating tasks in Active Directory and Exchange, this chapter provides a detailed guide to harnessing the full potential of PowerShell in the Microsoft ecosystem.

Managing Windows Server with PowerShell.

- **Introduction to Server Management**: Understanding the role of PowerShell in managing Windows Server. This includes tasks like server setup, role configuration, performance monitoring, and updates.

- **Practical Examples**: Demonstrating how PowerShell can be used to automate routine server management tasks.

Example

```
# Installing a Windows feature

Install-WindowsFeature -Name Web-Server -
IncludeManagementTools


# Checking server performance

Get-Counter -Counter "\Processor(_Total)\%
Processor Time" -SampleInterval 2 -  MaxSamples
10
```

- **Advanced Server Administration**: Delving into more complex scenarios like automated deployments, script-based network configuration, and security enhancements.

PowerShell and Active Directory.

- **Active Directory Automation**: PowerShell is a key tool for managing Active Directory. This includes user and group management, policy settings, and directory maintenance.
- **Scripting Examples**: Showcasing scripts for common Active Directory tasks like creating users, modifying group memberships, and managing organizational units.

Example

```
# Creating a new AD user
New-ADUser -Name "JohnDoe" -GivenName "John" -Surname "Doe" -SamAccountName "jdoe" -UserPrincipalName "jdoe@domain.com"
```

```
# Adding a user to a group
Add-ADGroupMember -Identity "HRDept" -Members "jdoe"
```

- **Bulk Operations**: Techniques for handling bulk operations in Active Directory using PowerShell, a vital skill for large-scale environments.

Automating tasks in Exchange and other Microsoft technologies.

- **Exchange Server Management**: PowerShell is instrumental in managing Exchange Server, from mailbox setup to complex mail flow rules.

- **Integration with Other Technologies**: Covering the use of PowerShell with other Microsoft technologies like SharePoint, SQL Server, and Azure services.

- **Automation Scripts**: Providing examples of automation scripts for repetitive tasks in Exchange and other services.

Example:

```
# Creating a new mailbox in Exchange

New-Mailbox -UserPrincipalName
"jdoe@domain.com" -Alias "jdoe" -Database
"MailboxDatabase01" -Name "JohnDoe" -
OrganizationalUnit "Users"

# Running a SQL query using PowerShell

Invoke-Sqlcmd -Query "SELECT * FROM
SalesLT.Product" -ServerInstance
"Server\Instance"
```

Conclusion

This chapter demonstrates the incredible synergy between PowerShell and Microsoft technologies, showcasing how PowerShell can be a game-changer in effectively managing and automating tasks across various Microsoft platforms. Whether you are an IT professional managing a Windows Server environment, an Active Directory administrator, or someone working with Exchange and other Microsoft services, this chapter offers valuable insights and practical examples to enhance your workflow and productivity using PowerShell.

Chapter 14: Integration with APIs and External Tools

In this chapter, we explore the versatile capabilities of PowerShell in interfacing with external APIs, leveraging the .NET Framework, and integrating with various tools and services. This integration extends PowerShell's functionality beyond traditional system management, allowing it to interact with a wide range of external resources, making it an invaluable tool for modern technology professionals.

Using PowerShell to interact with REST APIs.

- **Basics of REST API Interaction**:
  Understanding how PowerShell can be used to send HTTP requests to REST APIs. This includes handling various HTTP methods like GET, POST, PUT, and DELETE.

- **Authenticating and Consuming APIs**:
  Demonstrating how to authenticate to APIs using tokens or basic authentication and how to consume the data returned by these APIs.

Example

```
# Sending a GET request to a REST API

$response = Invoke-RestMethod -Uri
"https://api.example.com/data" -Method Get -
Headers @{Authorization = "Bearer
YourTokenHere"}


# Parsing JSON response

$data = $response | ConvertFrom-Json
```

- **Practical API Use Cases**: Covering real-world scenarios where PowerShell scripts can automate interactions with web services, such as updating DNS records, posting messages to chat applications, or automating tasks in cloud services.

Leveraging .NET Framework classes.

- **PowerShell and .NET Integration**: Exploring how PowerShell seamlessly integrates with the .NET Framework, allowing scripts to use .NET classes and their methods.

- **Implementing .NET in PowerShell Scripts**: Providing examples of using .NET classes for enhanced functionality in PowerShell scripts, such as file handling, network operations, and data manipulation.

  Example

```
# Using .NET to read a file

$content =
[System.IO.File]::ReadAllText("C:\path\to\your\file.txt
")
```

- **Advanced Scripting Techniques:** Delving into more complex scripting scenarios that leverage the full potential of .NET classes in PowerShell.

Integration with external tools and services.

- **Extending PowerShell's Reach**: Discussing the integration of PowerShell with other tools and platforms, enhancing its utility in a diverse range of environments.

- **Scripting for Tool Automation**: Showcasing how PowerShell can automate tasks in software like SQL Server, VMware, and various network monitoring tools.

- **Custom Tool Integration**: Providing guidance on how to write PowerShell scripts that can invoke and manage third-party tools, services, and custom applications.

Example

```
# Invoking an external tool

Start-Process -FilePath "C:\Program Files\CustomTool\tool.exe" -ArgumentList "/arg1 /arg2"
```

Conclusion

Chapter 14 equips you with the knowledge to extend PowerShell's capabilities far beyond its native environment, harnessing the power of APIs, the .NET Framework, and external tools. By integrating these diverse elements, PowerShell becomes a versatile and powerful scripting platform capable of automating and streamlining a vast array of tasks, making it an indispensable tool for tech professionals in various fields. Whether you're managing web services, interacting with external applications, or leveraging .NET's extensive library, this chapter provides the foundation and insights necessary for advanced PowerShell scripting.

Chapter 15: Advanced Topics and Best Practices

In this chapter, we'll delve into some of the more advanced aspects of PowerShell, focusing on workflows, scripting best practices, and staying current with the latest developments in the PowerShell ecosystem. This chapter is designed to elevate your PowerShell expertise to a higher level, emphasizing efficiency, maintainability, and community engagement.

Working with PowerShell workflows.

- **Introduction to Workflows**: Explore what PowerShell workflows are and how they differ from traditional scripts. Workflows in PowerShell allow for long-running processes, with capabilities such as parallel execution and persistence.

- **Creating and Managing Workflows**: Learn the syntax and structure of workflows, including how to define, execute, and manage them effectively.

Example

```
# Defining a simple workflow

workflow Get-SystemInfo {

    Get-Process

    Get-Service

}
# Executing the workflow

Get-SystemInfo
```

- **Use Cases for Workflows**: Discuss scenarios where workflows are particularly useful, such as in large-scale automation tasks and operations requiring robust error handling and recovery.

Best practices for scripting.

- **Writing Maintainable Code**: Focus on writing clear, maintainable PowerShell scripts. This includes using descriptive variable names, proper indentation, and commenting.

- **Error Handling**: Emphasize the importance of robust error handling using try-catch blocks and custom error messages to make scripts more reliable and user-friendly.

- **Modular Script Design**: Encourage the design of modular scripts. Break down scripts into functions and modules to enhance reusability and readability.

Example

```
# Example of a modular function
function Get-NetworkStatus {
    param ([string]$computerName)
    Test-Connection -ComputerName $computerName -Count 2 -Quiet
}
```

- **Performance Optimization**: Tips for optimizing script performance, such as using efficient loops, minimizing the use of resource-intensive cmdlets, and leveraging asynchronous operations.

Keeping up-to-date with PowerShell updates and community resources.

- **Staying Current with Updates**: Discuss the importance of keeping up-to-date with the latest PowerShell versions, including how to update PowerShell and the benefits of using the latest features and security enhancements.

- **Leveraging Community Resources**: Highlight the wealth of community resources available to PowerShell users. This includes forums, blogs, official documentation, and GitHub repositories.

- **Engaging with the PowerShell Community**: Encourage active participation in the PowerShell community, such as contributing to open-source projects, attending webinars and conferences, and networking with other PowerShell professionals.

- **Learning from Real-World Examples**: Showcase how real-world script examples from the community can be valuable learning resources. Provide guidance on how to adapt these examples to suit individual needs and environments.

Conclusion

Chapter 15 aims to provide you with advanced insights and practical advice to refine your PowerShell skills. By embracing workflows, adhering to best practices in scripting, and staying engaged with the community and latest updates, you'll be well-equipped to tackle complex tasks and contribute effectively to the evolving world of PowerShell. This chapter serves as a guide to not only enhancing your technical proficiency but also to becoming a proactive member of the PowerShell community.

Chapter 16: Real World Examples of PowerShell script

Report of disk space usage on all drives of a system, and then emailing this report

A common task many system administrators might perform generating a report of disk space usage on all drives of a system, and then emailing this report to the administrator. This script demonstrates several PowerShell capabilities, including system information retrieval, formatting data, and using PowerShell's built-in SMTP client to send an email.

```
# PowerShell script to report disk space and send an email

# Function to get disk space info

function Get-DiskSpaceReport {

    Get-PSDrive -PSProvider FileSystem |

    Select-Object Name,
    @{Name="Used(GB)";Expression={"{0:N2}" -f
    ($_.Used /      1GB)}},
    @{Name="Free(GB)";Expression={"{0:N2}" -f
    ($_.Free / 1GB)}},
    @{Name="Total(GB)";Expression={"{0:N2}" -f
    ($_.Used / 1GB + $_.Free / 1GB)}}

}
```

```
# Email parameters

$smtpServer = "smtp.yourdomain.com"

$smtpFrom = "admin@yourdomain.com"

$smtpTo = "admin@yourdomain.com"

$smtpSubject = "Disk Space Report - $(Get-Date -
Format 'MM/dd/yyyy')"

$smtpBody = (Get-DiskSpaceReport | Out-String)


# SMTP settings for sending the email

$smtp = New-Object
Net.Mail.SmtpClient($smtpServer)

$msg = New-Object
Net.Mail.MailMessage($smtpFrom, $smtpTo,
$smtpSubject, $smtpBody)

# Send the email

$smtp.Send($msg)
```

This script performs the following actions:

1. **Get-DiskSpaceReport Function**: Defines a function
   to get disk space information for all filesystem
   drives on the machine. It uses **Get-PSDrive** to get
   the drive information and then formats the output
   to show the used, free, and total space in gigabytes.

2. **Email Parameters**: Sets up the necessary parameters for sending the email, including the SMTP server, sender's and recipient's email addresses, subject, and body of the email. The body of the email is generated by calling the **Get-DiskSpaceReport** function and converting its output to a string.

3. **Sending the Email**: Creates an SMTP client object and a Mail message object with the parameters defined earlier. Then it sends the email using the **Send** method of the SMTP client.

This script can be scheduled to run at regular intervals using a task scheduler. Before running this script, you'll need to modify the SMTP server details and email addresses according to your environment.

Please note, running scripts that send emails automatically should be done with caution, ensuring they comply with your organization's IT policies and email usage guidelines.

PowerShell script that automates the process of backing up

PowerShell script that automates the process of backing up a list of specified directories to a backup location. This script can be particularly useful for routine backups of important folders, such as user data or configuration files. It demonstrates file manipulation, conditional logic, and basic error handling in PowerShell.

```powershell
# PowerShell script for directory backups


# List of directories to backup

$sourceDirectories = @("C:\Users\User\Documents", "C:\Work\Data")


# Backup destination

$backupDestination = "D:\Backups"


# Current date for backup folder naming

$currentDate = Get-Date -Format "yyyyMMdd"


# Function to perform backup

function Backup-Directories {
```

```powershell
param (
    [string[]]$sources,
    [string]$destination
)


foreach ($source in $sources) {
    # Create a unique directory for each backup
    $backupFolder = Join-Path -Path $destination -ChildPath ("$(Split-Path -Leaf $source)_$currentDate")


    # Check if source directory exists
    if (Test-Path -Path $source) {
        try {
            # Copying the directory
            Write-Host "Backing up $source to $backupFolder"
Copy-Item -Path $source -Destination $backupFolder -Recurse -ErrorAction Stop
            Write-Host "Backup completed for $source"
        } catch {
    Write-Host "Error backing up $source: $_"
```

```
                }

        } else {

                Write-Host "Source directory not found:
        $source"

                }

        }

}


# Call the backup function

Backup-Directories -sources $sourceDirectories -
destination $backupDestination
```

This script performs the following actions:

1. **Defining Directories**: It first defines a list of source directories that need to be backed up and a destination path where the backups will be stored.
2. **Backup Function**: The script then defines a **Backup-Directories** function. This function takes the source directories and the backup destination as parameters.
3. **Iterating and Backing Up**: Within the function, it iterates through each source directory, checks if it exists, and then copies it to the backup destination. The backup folder for each source directory is named uniquely by appending the current date.

4. **Error Handling**: The script includes basic error handling to catch any issues that occur during the backup process, such as permission issues or disk space problems.
5. **Executing the Backup**: Finally, the script calls the **Backup-Directories** function with the specified source directories and backup destination.

This kind of script is useful for regular backups and can be scheduled to run at specific intervals using a task scheduler. Adjust the source directories and backup destination path according to your requirements before running the script. Remember to test it in a safe environment first to ensure it works as expected.

PowerShell script that retrieves all the file shares from a list of servers in your Active Directory and outputs the information to a text file.

PowerShell script that retrieves all the file shares from a list of servers in your Active Directory and outputs the information to a text file. This script can be particularly useful for network administrators who need to audit or document the file shares across their network.

```
# PowerShell script to get file shares from Active Directory servers and output to a text file


# Import Active Directory module

Import-Module ActiveDirectory


# Define the list of servers to query for shared folders

# Replace with your actual server names or fetch dynamically from AD

$servers = @("Server1", "Server2", "Server3")


# Output file path
```

```powershell
$outputFilePath =
"C:\path\to\output\FileSharesReport.txt"


# Function to get shared folders from a server

function Get-SharedFolders {

    param (

        [string]$serverName

    )


# Retrieve and return the shared folders from the server

Get-WmiObject -Class Win32_Share -ComputerName
    $serverName | Where-Object { $_.Type -eq 0 }

    }


    # Create or clear the output file

    if (Test-Path -Path $outputFilePath) {

        Clear-Content -Path $outputFilePath

    } else {

        New-Item -Path $outputFilePath -ItemType File

    }


    # Iterate over each server and get shared folders
```

```powershell
foreach ($server in $servers) {

  Write-Host "Getting shared folders from
$server..."

  try {

    $shares = Get-SharedFolders -serverName
$server

    foreach ($share in $shares) {

      $shareInfo = "$server`: $($share.Name) -
$($share.Path)"

      Write-Output $shareInfo | Out-File -FilePath
$outputFilePath -Append

    }

  } catch {

Write-Host "Could not retrieve shares from $server:
$_"

    $errorMessage = "Error: Could not retrieve
shares from $server: $_"

    Write-Output $errorMessage | Out-File -
FilePath $outputFilePath -Append

  }

}


Write-Host "File shares report generated at
$outputFilePath"
```

In this script:

1. **Import Active Directory Module**: The script begins by importing the Active Directory module to work with AD-related cmdlets.
2. **Servers List**: We define a list of servers to check for shared folders. This list can be customized or dynamically generated based on your AD setup.
3. **Output File Path**: Define the path where the output file will be saved.
4. **Get-SharedFolders Function**: This function uses **Get-WmiObject** to query each server for shared folders (**Win32_Share** class).
5. **Output File Initialization**: The script checks if the output file already exists. If it does, it clears the content; if not, it creates a new file.
6. **Iterating and Writing Output**: The script iterates over each server, retrieves the shared folder information, and writes it to the output file. It appends each new entry to ensure all data is captured.
7. **Error Handling**: Any errors encountered during the execution are caught and written to both the console and the output file.

Before running the script, ensure the output file path is correctly set, and you have the required permissions to access the servers and write to the specified path. Also, test the script in a controlled environment first to ensure it works as expected.

Removing user accounts that have been disabled for a certain period of time.

It's a common practice to periodically clean up Active Directory by removing user accounts that have been disabled for a certain period of time. The following PowerShell script automates this task. It searches for user accounts that have been disabled and have not been modified within the last 90 days (or any other period you choose), and then removes these accounts from Active Directory.

Before running this script, please make sure you have the necessary permissions and that you execute it in a test environment first to validate its behavior, as deleting user accounts is an irreversible operation.

```
# PowerShell script to remove disabled users from
Active Directory


# Import Active Directory module

Import-Module ActiveDirectory


# Define the time period (90 days in this example)

$daysInactive = 90

$inactiveDate = (Get-Date).Adddays(-$daysInactive)
```

```powershell
# Search for disabled users who haven't been modified
in the last 90 days

$disabledUsers = Get-ADUser -Filter {(Enabled -eq
$false) -and (whenChanged -lt $inactiveDate)}    -
Properties whenChanged


# Iterate over each user and remove them

foreach ($user in $disabledUsers) {

    try {

        # Removing the user from Active Directory

        Remove-ADUser -Identity $user.DistinguishedName -
Confirm:$false

        Write-Host "Removed user:
$($user.SamAccountName)"

    } catch {

        Write-Host "Error removing user
$($user.SamAccountName): $_"

    }

}


Write-Host "Cleanup completed."
```

In this script:

1. **Importing Active Directory Module**: The script starts by importing the Active Directory module, which is required for AD cmdlets.
2. **Defining Time Period**: It defines a variable for the number of days to check for inactivity (90 days in this case). The **$inactiveDate** variable holds the date before which the user accounts must have been modified to be considered for deletion.
3. **Finding Disabled Users**: The script uses **Get-ADUser** to find all users who are disabled (**Enabled -eq $false**) and who haven't been modified since **$inactiveDate**.
4. **Removing Users**: It then iterates through each user found and uses the **Remove-ADUser** cmdlet to delete the user from Active Directory. The -**Confirm:$false** flag is used to bypass the confirmation prompt for each deletion.
5. **Error Handling**: The script includes error handling to catch and report any issues that might occur during the removal process.
6. **Logging**: For each user that is removed, the script logs the action to the console.

Remember to adjust the **$daysInactive** value as per your organizational policies and test this script thoroughly in a non-production environment before using it in live settings. This script can have significant impacts if used incorrectly.

Chapter 17: Security Concerns

Using PowerShell, while powerful and efficient for managing and automating tasks across systems, raises several security concerns. These concerns are primarily due to PowerShell's deep access to internal system components and its ability to interface with the .NET Framework. Here are some key security concerns associated with using PowerShell:

1. **Malicious Scripts and Commands**: PowerShell can execute complex scripts and commands, which can be a vector for malware or malicious activities. Attackers can use PowerShell to gain unauthorized access, exfiltrate data, or execute harmful actions within a network.

2. **Bypassing Security Software**: PowerShell scripts can sometimes bypass traditional antivirus or security software, as these scripts are often seen as legitimate administrative tools by the system.

3. **PowerShell Remoting**: While PowerShell remoting is a powerful feature for administrators, it can also be exploited by attackers to remotely execute commands on target machines.

4. **Execution Policy Vulnerabilities**: PowerShell's execution policy is designed to prevent

unintended script execution. However, these policies are not security boundaries. Malicious users can bypass execution policies to run unauthorized scripts.

5. **Logging and Auditing Challenges**: PowerShell's extensive capabilities can make it difficult to track and audit activities. While PowerShell does have logging features, attackers can disable or manipulate these logs.

6. **Fileless Attacks**: PowerShell can execute scripts directly from memory (fileless execution), making it harder to detect and trace malicious activities.

7. **Privilege Escalation**: PowerShell scripts can be used for privilege escalation by exploiting system vulnerabilities or misconfigurations.

8. **Embedded Scripts**: PowerShell scripts can be embedded in other file types, such as Office documents, making it a vector for phishing and other social engineering attacks.

9. **Obfuscation Techniques**: Attackers can use advanced obfuscation techniques to hide the purpose of PowerShell scripts, making detection by security teams more difficult.

10. **Credential Theft**: PowerShell can access sensitive system areas, including credential

stores, increasing the risk of credential theft or misuse.

To mitigate these risks, it's important to:

- Regularly update PowerShell and the underlying .NET framework to the latest versions.
- Implement robust logging and monitoring, including the use of PowerShell logging features like script block logging and transcription.
- Restrict PowerShell remoting to trusted users and configure it to use secure authentication methods.
- Employ the principle of least privilege, ensuring users and scripts only have the necessary permissions.
- Use advanced threat detection tools that can identify malicious PowerShell activity.
- Educate users and administrators about the safe use of PowerShell and the risks associated with its misuse.

By understanding these security concerns and implementing best practices, organizations can safely utilize PowerShell's powerful capabilities while minimizing potential risks.

Enhanced Security Concerns with PowerShell

1. **Advanced Persistent Threats (APTs)**:
   - APTs often use PowerShell as part of their attack chain due to its deep system integration and ability to run complex scripts. These threats can remain undetected for long periods, causing significant harm.

2. **Code Injection and Script Tampering**:
   - PowerShell allows the execution of dynamic code, which can be exploited to inject malicious code into scripts. Tampering with legitimate scripts can lead to unauthorized actions.

3. **Lateral Movement within Networks**:
   - PowerShell can be used by attackers to move laterally across a network after gaining initial access, exploiting the trust relationships between machines.

4. **Use in Multi-stage Attack Vectors**:
   - In complex cyber attacks, PowerShell might be used in one or more stages, such as delivering a payload, reconnaissance, or data exfiltration.

5. **Decrypting Secure Content**:
   - PowerShell has the ability to interact with Windows API and system internals, potentially allowing attackers to decrypt or access sensitive data.

6. **Use in 'Living off the Land' Strategies**:
   - Attackers often use built-in tools like PowerShell in 'living off the land' strategies to avoid detection, as these tools don't arouse immediate suspicion.

Mitigation Strategies

1. **Restrict PowerShell Access**:
   - Limit PowerShell usage to users and accounts that require it for legitimate tasks. Implement Role-Based Access Control (RBAC) where possible.

2. **Enhanced Monitoring and Logging**:
   - Enable enhanced logging features in PowerShell, such as Module Logging, Script Block Logging, and Transcription. Use security information and event management (SIEM) systems to monitor for suspicious activity.

3. **Endpoint Protection Solutions**:
   - Use advanced endpoint protection platforms (EPP) that include behavior-based detection capabilities to identify malicious PowerShell activity.

4. **Application Whitelisting**:
   - Implement application whitelisting tools like AppLocker or Windows Defender Application Control (WDAC) to control script

execution and prevent unauthorized scripts from running.

5. **Regular Audits and Reviews**:
   - Conduct regular audits of PowerShell usage and scripts in your environment. Review and update security policies regularly.

6. **Training and Awareness**:
   - Educate IT staff and end-users about the potential misuse of PowerShell and encourage security best practices.

7. **Network Segmentation**:
   - Implement network segmentation and microsegmentation to limit lateral movement possibilities for attackers.
   -

8. **Use of Just Enough Administration (JEA)**:
   - JEA is a PowerShell toolkit that helps in configuring and using PowerShell in a way that reduces security risks by limiting the capabilities based on the specific tasks a user needs to perform.

By combining these strategies, organizations can significantly reduce the security risks associated with PowerShell while still leveraging its powerful capabilities for system administration and automation. It's important to strike a balance between usability and security to ensure that PowerShell remains a valuable tool without becoming a liability.

Getting your Shell on
with Powershell

By: Michael Neumann

Published by Mediaguruz Publishing at Mediaguruz.com